Mug'ems

Meals & More

Give'em & Bake'em ~ Recipes in a Mug!

Printed in the United States of America
by G&R Publishing Co.

Published By:

507 Industrial Street
Waverly, IA 50677

ISBN-13: 978-1-56383-478-3
ISBN-10: 1-56383-478-2
Item #3019

Chicken & Rice Casserole Mix

Chicken & Rice Casserole Mix

⅓ C. instant rice
1 tsp. dried celery flakes
¼ tsp. dried onion flakes

1 tsp. dried chives
1 (5 oz.) can chunk chicken

In a small bowl, combine rice, celery flakes, onion flakes and chives. Mix well, place in a sandwich-size bag and seal. Place can of chicken in a mug and top with sealed bag. Make sure the mug holds a volume of at least 1½ cups.

Decorate mug and attach a gift tag with the directions on how to prepare the casserole.

Chicken & Rice Casserole

Chicken & Rice Casserole Mix
½ C. water
1 T. butter
2 T. shredded Cheddar cheese

Empty Chicken & Rice Casserole Mix into a mug. Add drained chicken from can to ingredients in mug. In a small saucepan over medium heat, bring water and butter to a boil and pour over ingredients in mug. Mix well and let stand for 5 to 8 minutes. Top with Cheddar cheese and heat in microwave until cheese is melted.

For a quality black and white reproduction, photocopy the above tag.
Any of the color tags may also be photocopied for additional gifts.

Chicken & Rice Casserole

Chicken & Rice Casserole Mix
½ C. water
1 T. butter
2 T. shredded Cheddar cheese

Empty Chicken & Rice Casserole Mix into a mug. Add drained chicken from can to ingredients in mug. In a small saucepan over medium heat, bring water and butter to a boil and pour over ingredients in mug. Mix well and let stand for 5 to 8 minutes. Top with Cheddar cheese and heat in microwave until cheese is melted.

Chicken & Rice Casserole

Chicken & Rice Casserole Mix
½ C. water
1 T. butter
2 T. shredded Cheddar cheese

Empty Chicken & Rice Casserole Mix into a mug. Add drained chicken from can to ingredients in mug. In a small saucepan over medium heat, bring water and butter to a boil and pour over ingredients in mug. Mix well and let stand for 5 to 8 minutes. Top with Cheddar cheese and heat in microwave until cheese is melted.

Chicken & Rice Casserole

Chicken & Rice Casserole Mix
½ C. water
1 T. butter
2 T. shredded Cheddar cheese

Empty Chicken & Rice Casserole Mix into a mug. Add drained chicken from can to ingredients in mug. In a small saucepan over medium heat, bring water and butter to a boil and pour over ingredients in mug. Mix well and let stand for 5 to 8 minutes. Top with Cheddar cheese and heat in microwave until cheese is melted.

Chicken & Rice Casserole

Chicken & Rice Casserole Mix
½ C. water
1 T. butter
2 T. shredded Cheddar cheese

Empty Chicken & Rice Casserole Mix into a mug. Add drained chicken from can to ingredients in mug. In a small saucepan over medium heat, bring water and butter to a boil and pour over ingredients in mug. Mix well and let stand for 5 to 8 minutes. Top with Cheddar cheese and heat in microwave until cheese is melted.

Hearty Ranch
Potatoes Mix

Hearty Ranch Potatoes Mix

⅔ C. instant mashed potato flakes

1 T. dry ranch dressing mix

1 T. bacon bits

1 tsp. dried chives

In a small bowl, combine above ingredients. Mix well, place in a sandwich-size bag and seal. Place sealed bag in a mug. Make sure the mug holds a volume of at least 1½ cups.

Decorate mug and attach a gift tag with the directions on how to prepare the potatoes.

Hearty Ranch Potatoes

Hearty Ranch Potatoes Mix
½ C. plus 1 T. water
⅓ C. milk
1 T. butter or margarine

Empty Hearty Ranch Potatoes Mix into a mug. In small saucepan over medium heat, place water, milk and butter. Bring to a low simmer and pour over ingredients in mug. Mix well, cover and let stand for 5 minutes. Fluff lightly with a fork. If desired, top with shredded cheese or bacon bits.

For a quality black and white reproduction, photocopy the above tag. Any of the color tags may also be photocopied for additional gifts.

Hearty Ranch Potatoes

Hearty Ranch Potatoes Mix
½ C. plus 1 T. water
⅓ C. milk
1 T. butter or margarine

Empty Hearty Ranch Potatoes Mix into a mug. In small saucepan over medium heat, place water, milk and butter. Bring to a low simmer and pour over ingredients in mug. Mix well, cover and let stand for 5 minutes. Fluff lightly with a fork. If desired, top with shredded cheese or bacon bits.

Hearty Ranch Potatoes

Hearty Ranch Potatoes Mix
½ C. plus 1 T. water
⅓ C. milk
1 T. butter or margarine

Empty Hearty Ranch Potatoes Mix into a mug. In small saucepan over medium heat, place water, milk and butter. Bring to a low simmer and pour over ingredients in mug. Mix well, cover and let stand for 5 minutes. Fluff lightly with a fork. If desired, top with shredded cheese or bacon bits.

Hearty Ranch Potatoes

Hearty Ranch Potatoes Mix
½ C. plus 1 T. water
⅓ C. milk
1 T. butter or margarine

Empty Hearty Ranch Potatoes Mix into a mug. In small saucepan over medium heat, place water, milk and butter. Bring to a low simmer and pour over ingredients in mug. Mix well, cover and let stand for 5 minutes. Fluff lightly with a fork. If desired, top with shredded cheese or bacon bits.

HEARTY RANCH POTATOES

Hearty Ranch Potatoes Mix
½ C. plus 1 T. water
⅓ C. milk
1 T. butter or margarine

Empty Hearty Ranch Potatoes Mix into a mug. In small saucepan over medium heat, place water, milk and butter. Bring to a low simmer and pour over ingredients in mug. Mix well, cover and let stand for 5 minutes. Fluff lightly with a fork. If desired, top with shredded cheese or bacon bits.

Nutty
Oatmeal Mix

Nutty Oatmeal Mix

¾ C. old-fashioned oats
1 T. powdered coffee creamer
1½ T. chopped pecans or walnuts

1 T. brown sugar
1½ T. raisins
¼ tsp. cinnamon
Pinch of salt

In a small bowl, combine above ingredients. Mix well, place in a sandwich-size bag and seal. Place sealed bag in a mug. Make sure the mug holds a volume of at least 1½ cups.

Decorate mug and attach a gift tag with the directions on how to prepare the oatmeal.

Nutty Oatmeal

Nutty Oatmeal Mix
1 C. water
1 T. butter
¼ tsp. vanilla

Empty Nutty Oatmeal Mix into a mug. Stir in water, butter and vanilla. Heat oatmeal mixture in microwave for 1 to 2 minutes. Stir and let cool slightly. If desired, top with fresh fruit before enjoying.

For a quality black and white reproduction, photocopy the above tag.
Any of the color tags may also be photocopied for additional gifts.

NUTTY OATMEAL

Nutty Oatmeal Mix
1 C. water
1 T. butter
¼ tsp. vanilla

Empty Nutty Oatmeal Mix into a mug. Stir in water, butter and vanilla. Heat oatmeal mixture in microwave for 1 to 2 minutes. Stir and let cool slightly. If desired, top with fresh fruit before enjoying.

Nutty Oatmeal

Nutty Oatmeal Mix
1 C. water
1 T. butter
¼ tsp. vanilla

Empty Nutty Oatmeal Mix into a mug. Stir in water, butter and vanilla. Heat oatmeal mixture in microwave for 1 to 2 minutes. Stir and let cool slightly. If desired, top with fresh fruit before enjoying.

Nutty Oatmeal

Nutty Oatmeal Mix
1 C. water
1 T. butter
¼ tsp. vanilla

Empty Nutty Oatmeal Mix into a mug. Stir in water, butter and vanilla. Heat oatmeal mixture in microwave for 1 to 2 minutes. Stir and let cool slightly. If desired, top with fresh fruit before enjoying.

Nutty Oatmeal

Nutty Oatmeal Mix
1 C. water
1 T. butter
¼ tsp. vanilla

Empty Nutty Oatmeal Mix into a mug. Stir in water, butter and vanilla. Heat oatmeal mixture in microwave for 1 to 2 minutes. Stir and let cool slightly. If desired, top with fresh fruit before enjoying.

Mexican
Lasagna Mix

Mexican Lasagna Mix

½ tsp. dried onion flakes
½ tsp. dried green bell
   pepper
Pinch of garlic powder
½ tsp. dried oregano

1 T. grated Parmesan
   cheese
¼ C. crushed corn
   tortilla chips

In small bowl, combine onion flakes, dried bell pepper, garlic powder, oregano and Parmesan cheese. Mix well, place in a sandwich-size bag and seal. Place crushed tortilla chips in a separate bag and seal. Place sealed bags in a mug. Make sure the mug holds a volume of at least 1½ cups.

Decorate mug and attach a gift tag with the directions on how to prepare the lasagna.

Mexican Lasagna

½ C. ground beef
Mexican Lasagna Mix
¼ C. pizza sauce
¼ C. cottage cheese
⅓ C. shredded Cheddar
   cheese

Preheat oven to 350°. In small saucepan over medium heat, cook ground beef and drain off fat. Add Mexican Lasagna Mix and pizza sauce to meat and stir well. In a separate bowl, combine cottage cheese and Cheddar cheese. In lightly greased mug, layer cooked ground beef, crushed tortilla chips from bag and cheese mixture. Repeat layers. Bake for 15 to 20 minutes.

For a quality black and white reproduction, photocopy the above tag.
Any of the color tags may also be photocopied for additional gifts.

Mexican Lasagna

½ C. ground beef
Mexican Lasagna Mix
¼ C. pizza sauce
¼ C. cottage cheese
⅓ C. shredded Cheddar
cheese

Preheat oven to 350°. In small saucepan over medium heat, cook ground beef and drain off fat. Add Mexican Lasagna Mix and pizza sauce to meat and stir well. In a separate bowl, combine cottage cheese and Cheddar cheese. In lightly greased mug, layer cooked ground beef, crushed tortilla chips from bag and cheese mixture. Repeat layers. Bake for 15 to 20 minutes.

MEXICAN LASAGNA

½ C. ground beef
Mexican Lasagna Mix
¼ C. pizza sauce
¼ C. cottage cheese
⅓ C. shredded Cheddar
cheese

Preheat oven to 350°. In small saucepan over medium heat, cook ground beef and drain off fat. Add Mexican Lasagna Mix and pizza sauce to meat and stir well. In a separate bowl, combine cottage cheese and Cheddar cheese. In lightly greased mug, layer cooked ground beef, crushed tortilla chips from bag and cheese mixture. Repeat layers. Bake for 15 to 20 minutes.

Mexican Lasagna

½ C. ground beef
Mexican Lasagna Mix
¼ C. pizza sauce
¼ C. cottage cheese
⅓ C. shredded Cheddar
cheese

Preheat oven to 350°. In small saucepan over medium heat, cook ground beef and drain off fat. Add Mexican Lasagna Mix and pizza sauce to meat and stir well. In a separate bowl, combine cottage cheese and Cheddar cheese. In lightly greased mug, layer cooked ground beef, crushed tortilla chips from bag and cheese mixture. Repeat layers. Bake for 15 to 20 minutes.

Mexican Lasagna

½ C. ground beef
Mexican Lasagna Mix
¼ C. pizza sauce
¼ C. cottage cheese
⅓ C. shredded Cheddar
cheese

Preheat oven to 350°. In small saucepan over medium heat, cook ground beef and drain off fat. Add Mexican Lasagna Mix and pizza sauce to meat and stir well. In a separate bowl, combine cottage cheese and Cheddar cheese. In lightly greased mug, layer cooked ground beef, crushed tortilla chips from bag and cheese mixture. Repeat layers. Bake for 15 to 20 minutes.

Golden Fruit
Compote Mix

Golden Fruit Compote Mix

2 T. pitted dried plums (prunes), quartered

2 T. sugar

3 T. dried cherries

3 T. golden raisins

¼ tsp. cinnamon

In a small bowl, combine above ingredients. Mix well, place in a sandwich-size bag and seal. Place sealed bag in a mug. Make sure the mug holds a volume of at least 1½ cups.

Decorate mug and attach a gift tag with the directions on how to prepare the fruit compote.

Golden Fruit Compote

Golden Fruit Compote Mix

½ C. peeled, cored and chopped apple

1 T. butter or margarine, melted

⅓ c. apple juice

Preheat oven to 350°. Place Golden Fruit Compote Mix in lightly greased mug. Stir in chopped apple, melted butter and apple juice. Loosely cover with aluminum foil and bake for 18 to 22 minutes. Enjoy!

For a quality black and white reproduction, photocopy the above tag. Any of the color tags may also be photocopied for additional gifts.

Golden Fruit Compote

Golden Fruit Compote Mix
½ C. peeled, cored and
  chopped apple
1 T. butter or margarine,
  melted
⅓ C. apple juice

Preheat oven to 350°. Place Golden Fruit Compote Mix in lightly greased mug. Stir in chopped apple, melted butter and apple juice. Loosely cover with aluminum foil and bake for 18 to 22 minutes. Enjoy!

Golden Fruit Compote

Golden Fruit Compote Mix
½ C. peeled, cored and
  chopped apple
1 T. butter or margarine,
  melted
⅓ C. apple juice

Preheat oven to 350°. Place Golden Fruit Compote Mix in lightly greased mug. Stir in chopped apple, melted butter and apple juice. Loosely cover with aluminum foil and bake for 18 to 22 minutes. Enjoy!

Golden Fruit Compote

Golden Fruit Compote Mix
½ C. peeled, cored and
  chopped apple
1 T. butter or margarine,
  melted
⅓ C. apple juice

Preheat oven to 350°. Place Golden Fruit Compote Mix in lightly greased mug. Stir in chopped apple, melted butter and apple juice. Loosely cover with aluminum foil and bake for 18 to 22 minutes. Enjoy!

Golden Fruit Compote

Golden Fruit Compote Mix
½ C. peeled, cored and
  chopped apple
1 T. butter or margarine,
  melted
⅓ C. apple juice

Preheat oven to 350°. Place Golden Fruit Compote Mix in lightly greased mug. Stir in chopped apple, melted butter and apple juice. Loosely cover with aluminum foil and bake for 18 to 22 minutes. Enjoy!

Grits & Cheese Casserole Mix

Grits & Cheese Casserole Mix

2 T. grits
½ T. dried onion flakes
1 T. bacon bits

1 tsp. dried chives
½ tsp. salt
Pinch of black pepper

In a small bowl, combine the above ingredients. Mix well, place in a sandwich-size bag and seal. Place sealed bag in a mug. Make sure the mug holds a volume of at least 1½ cups.

Decorate mug and attach a gift tag with the directions on how to prepare the casserole.

Grits & Cheese Casserole

Grits & Cheese Casserole Mix
⅔ C. water
1 small egg
2 T. shredded Cheddar cheese

Preheat oven to 350°. Empty Grits & Cheese Casserole Mix into a mug. In small saucepan over medium heat, bring water to a boil and pour over ingredients in mug. Stir well and let mixture stand for 5 minutes. In a small bowl, lightly beat egg. Add beaten egg and Cheddar cheese to mug. Stir and bake for 20 to 25 minutes.

For a quality black and white reproduction, photocopy the above tag. Any of the color tags may also be photocopied for additional gifts.

Grits & Cheese Casserole

Grits & Cheese Casserole
  Mix
⅔ C. water
1 small egg
2 T. shredded Cheddar
  cheese

Preheat oven to 350°. Empty Grits & Cheese Casserole Mix into a mug. In small saucepan over medium heat, bring water to a boil and pour over ingredients in mug. Stir well and let mixture stand for 5 minutes. In a small bowl, lightly beat egg. Add beaten egg and Cheddar cheese to mug. Stir and bake for 20 to 25 minutes.

Grits & Cheese Casserole

Grits & Cheese Casserole
  Mix
⅔ C. water
1 small egg
2 T. shredded Cheddar
  cheese

Preheat oven to 350°. Empty Grits & Cheese Casserole Mix into a mug. In small saucepan over medium heat, bring water to a boil and pour over ingredients in mug. Stir well and let mixture stand for 5 minutes. In a small bowl, lightly beat egg. Add beaten egg and Cheddar cheese to mug. Stir and bake for 20 to 25 minutes.

Grits & Cheese Casserole

Grits & Cheese Casserole
  Mix
⅔ C. water
1 small egg
2 T. shredded Cheddar
  cheese

Preheat oven to 350°. Empty Grits & Cheese Casserole Mix into a mug. In small saucepan over medium heat, bring water to a boil and pour over ingredients in mug. Stir well and let mixture stand for 5 minutes. In a small bowl, lightly beat egg. Add beaten egg and Cheddar cheese to mug. Stir and bake for 20 to 25 minutes.

GRITS & CHEESE CASSEROLE

Grits & Cheese Casserole
  Mix
⅔ C. water
1 small egg
2 T. shredded Cheddar
  cheese

Preheat oven to 350°. Empty Grits & Cheese Casserole Mix into a mug. In small saucepan over medium heat, bring water to a boil and pour over ingredients in mug. Stir well and let mixture stand for 5 minutes. In a small bowl, lightly beat egg. Add beaten egg and Cheddar cheese to mug. Stir and bake for 20 to 25 minutes.

Currant Almond

Currant Almond Rice Mix
1 T. butter
½ C. water

Empty Currant Almond Rice
a small saucepan over mediu
butter and water. Bring to a b
over ingredients in mug. Loos
aluminum foil and let mixture
minutes. Fluff lightly with a for

Currant Almond
Rice Mix

Currant Almond Rice Mix

½ C. instant rice
2 T. currants
1½ T. toasted sliced
   almonds

1½ tsp. instant chicken
   bouillon
1 tsp. dried celery flakes

In a small bowl, combine above ingredients. Mix well, place in a sandwich-size bag and seal. Place sealed bag in a mug. Make sure the mug holds a volume of at least 1½ cups.

Decorate mug and attach a gift tag with the directions on how to prepare the rice.

Currant Almond Rice

Currant Almond Rice Mix
1 T. butter
⅔ C. water

Empty Currant Almond Rice Mix into a mug. In a small saucepan over medium heat, combine butter and water. Bring to a boil and pour over ingredients in mug. Loosely cover with aluminum foil and let mixture stand for 6 to 10 minutes. Fluff lightly with a fork and enjoy.

For a quality black and white reproduction, photocopy the above tag. Any of the color tags may also be photocopied for additional gifts.

Currant Almond Rice

Currant Almond Rice Mix
1 T. butter
⅔ C. water

Empty Currant Almond Rice Mix into a mug. In a small saucepan over medium heat, combine butter and water. Bring to a boil and pour over ingredients in mug. Loosely cover with aluminum foil and let mixture stand for 6 to 10 minutes. Fluff lightly with a fork and enjoy.

Currant Almond Rice

Currant Almond Rice Mix
1 T. butter
⅔ C. water

Empty Currant Almond Rice Mix into a mug. In a small saucepan over medium heat, combine butter and water. Bring to a boil and pour over ingredients in mug. Loosely cover with aluminum foil and let mixture stand for 6 to 10 minutes. Fluff lightly with a fork and enjoy.

Currant Almond Rice

Currant Almond Rice Mix
1 T. butter
⅔ C. water

Empty Currant Almond Rice Mix into a mug. In a small saucepan over medium heat, combine butter and water. Bring to a boil and pour over ingredients in mug. Loosely cover with aluminum foil and let mixture stand for 6 to 10 minutes. Fluff lightly with a fork and enjoy.

Currant Almond Rice

Currant Almond Rice Mix
1 T. butter
⅔ C. water

Empty Currant Almond Rice Mix into a mug. In a small saucepan over medium heat, combine butter and water. Bring to a boil and pour over ingredients in mug. Loosely cover with aluminum foil and let mixture stand for 6 to 10 minutes. Fluff lightly with a fork and enjoy.

Pecan Chicken & Rice Salad Mix

Pecan Chicken & Rice Salad Mix

½ C. instant rice
1 tsp. instant chicken
    bouillon
1 T. raisins

1 T. chopped pecans
1 tsp. dried parsley flakes
1 (5 oz.) can chicken

In a small bowl, combine above ingredients. Mix well, place in a sandwich-size bag and seal. Place can of chicken in a mug and top with sealed bag. Make sure the mug holds a volume of at least 1½ cups.

Decorate mug and attach a gift tag with the directions on how to prepare the rice salad.

Pecan Chicken & Rice Salad

Pecan Chicken & Rice
    Salad Mix
⅓ C. water
2 T. orange juice
1 T. olive oil

Empty Pecan Chicken & Rice Salad Mix into a mug. In a small saucepan over medium heat, combine water, orange juice and oil. Bring to a boil and pour over ingredients in mug. Cover with aluminum foil and let mixture stand for 6 to 10 minutes. Add drained chicken from can to rice mixture and mix well. Enjoy!

For a quality black and white reproduction, photocopy the above tag. Any of the color tags may also be photocopied for additional gifts.

PECAN CHICKEN & RICE SALAD

Pecan Chicken & Rice
Salad Mix
⅓ C. water
2 T. orange juice
1 T. olive oil

Empty Pecan Chicken & Rice Salad Mix into a mug. In a small saucepan over medium heat, combine water, orange juice and oil. Bring to a boil and pour over ingredients in mug. Cover with aluminum foil and let mixture stand for 6 to 10 minutes. Add drained chicken from can to rice mixture and mix well. Enjoy!

Pecan Chicken & Rice Salad

Pecan Chicken & Rice
Salad Mix
⅓ C. water
2 T. orange juice
1 T. olive oil

Empty Pecan Chicken & Rice Salad Mix into a mug. In a small saucepan over medium heat, combine water, orange juice and oil. Bring to a boil and pour over ingredients in mug. Cover with aluminum foil and let mixture stand for 6 to 10 minutes. Add drained chicken from can to rice mixture and mix well. Enjoy!

Pecan Chicken & Rice Salad

Pecan Chicken & Rice
Salad Mix
⅓ C. water
2 T. orange juice
1 T. olive oil

Empty Pecan Chicken & Rice Salad Mix into a mug. In a small saucepan over medium heat, combine water, orange juice and oil. Bring to a boil and pour over ingredients in mug. Cover with aluminum foil and let mixture stand for 6 to 10 minutes. Add drained chicken from can to rice mixture and mix well. Enjoy!

Pecan Chicken & Rice Salad

Pecan Chicken & Rice
Salad Mix
⅓ C. water
2 T. orange juice
1 T. olive oil

Empty Pecan Chicken & Rice Salad Mix into a mug. In a small saucepan over medium heat, combine water, orange juice and oil. Bring to a boil and pour over ingredients in mug. Cover with aluminum foil and let mixture stand for 6 to 10 minutes. Add drained chicken from can to rice mixture and mix well. Enjoy!

Hot Chicken Salad Casserole Mix

Hot Chicken Salad Casserole Mix

½ C. dried, cubed bread or breadcrumbs
1 tsp. dried celery flakes
½ tsp. dried onion flakes
1 tsp. instant chicken bouillon
1 T. chopped walnuts
1 (5 oz.) can chunk chicken

In a small bowl, combine above ingredients. Mix well, place in a sandwich-size bag and seal. Place can of chicken in mug and top with sealed bag. Make sure the mug holds a volume of at least 1½ cups.

Decorate mug and attach a gift tag with the directions on how to prepare the casserole.

Hot Chicken Salad Casserole

1 T. butter, melted
1 T. water
1 T. sour cream
1 T. mayonnaise
Hot Chicken Salad Casserole Mix

Preheat oven to 350°. In a small bowl, combine drained chicken from can, melted butter, water, sour cream and mayonnaise. Add Hot Chicken Salad Casserole Mix to ingredients in bowl. Stir well and pour mixture into lightly greased mug. Cover with aluminum foil and bake for 16 to 20 minutes.

For a quality black and white reproduction, photocopy the above tag. Any of the color tags may also be photocopied for additional gifts.

Hot Chicken Salad Casserole

1 T. butter, melted
1 T. water
1 T. sour cream
1 T. mayonnaise
Hot Chicken Salad
  Casserole Mix

Preheat oven to 350°. In a small bowl, combine drained chicken from can, melted butter, water, sour cream and mayonnaise. Add Hot Chicken Salad Casserole Mix to ingredients in bowl. Stir well and pour mixture into lightly greased mug. Cover with aluminum foil and bake for 16 to 20 minutes.

Hot Chicken Salad Casserole

1 T. butter, melted
1 T. water
1 T. sour cream
1 T. mayonnaise
Hot Chicken Salad
  Casserole Mix

Preheat oven to 350°. In a small bowl, combine drained chicken from can, melted butter, water, sour cream and mayonnaise. Add Hot Chicken Salad Casserole Mix to ingredients in bowl. Stir well and pour mixture into lightly greased mug. Cover with aluminum foil and bake for 16 to 20 minutes.

Hot Chicken Salad Casserole

1 T. butter, melted
1 T. water
1 T. sour cream
1 T. mayonnaise
Hot Chicken Salad
  Casserole Mix

Preheat oven to 350°. In a small bowl, combine drained chicken from can, melted butter, water, sour cream and mayonnaise. Add Hot Chicken Salad Casserole Mix to ingredients in bowl. Stir well and pour mixture into lightly greased mug. Cover with aluminum foil and bake for 16 to 20 minutes.

Hot Chicken Salad Casserole

1 T. butter, melted
1 T. water
1 T. sour cream
1 T. mayonnaise
Hot Chicken Salad
  Casserole Mix

Preheat oven to 350°. In a small bowl, combine drained chicken from can, melted butter, water, sour cream and mayonnaise. Add Hot Chicken Salad Casserole Mix to ingredients in bowl. Stir well and pour mixture into lightly greased mug. Cover with aluminum foil and bake for 16 to 20 minutes.

Hash Brown Casserole

Preheat oven to 350°. Empty Hash Brown Casserole Mix into a mug. In small saucepan over medium heat, combine water and butter. Bring to a simmer and pour over ingredients in mug, stirring until well combined. Stir in sour cream. Cover with aluminum foil and bake for 20 to 25 minutes.

Hash Brown
Casserole Mix

Hash Brown Casserole Mix

1 C. dehydrated hash brown potatoes
2 T. chicken gravy mix

1 tsp. dried chives
1 T. bacon bits

In a small bowl, combine above ingredients. Mix well, place in a sandwich-size bag and seal. Place sealed bag in a mug. Make sure the mug holds a volume of at least 1½ cups.

Decorate mug and attach a gift tag with the directions on how to prepare the casserole.

Hash Brown Casserole

Hash Brown Casserole Mix
¾ C. water
1 T. butter
1 T. sour cream

Preheat oven to 350°. Empty Hash Brown Casserole Mix into a mug. In small saucepan over medium heat, combine water and butter. Bring to a simmer and pour over ingredients in mug, stirring until well combined. Stir in sour cream. Cover with aluminum foil and bake for 20 to 25 minutes.

For a quality black and white reproduction, photocopy the above tag. Any of the color tags may also be photocopied for additional gifts.

HASH BROWN CASSEROLE

Hash Brown Casserole Mix
¾ C. water
1 T. butter
1 T. sour cream

Preheat oven to 350°. Empty Hash Brown Casserole Mix into a mug. In small saucepan over medium heat, combine water and butter. Bring to a simmer and pour over ingredients in mug, stirring until well combined. Stir in sour cream. Cover with aluminum foil and bake for 20 to 25 minutes.

Hash Brown Casserole

Hash Brown Casserole Mix
¾ C. water
1 T. butter
1 T. sour cream

Preheat oven to 350°. Empty Hash Brown Casserole Mix into a mug. In small saucepan over medium heat, combine water and butter. Bring to a simmer and pour over ingredients in mug, stirring until well combined. Stir in sour cream. Cover with aluminum foil and bake for 20 to 25 minutes.

Hash Brown Casserole

Hash Brown Casserole Mix
¾ C. water
1 T. butter
1 T. sour cream

Preheat oven to 350°. Empty Hash Brown Casserole Mix into a mug. In small saucepan over medium heat, combine water and butter. Bring to a simmer and pour over ingredients in mug, stirring until well combined. Stir in sour cream. Cover with aluminum foil and bake for 20 to 25 minutes.

Hash Brown Casserole

Hash Brown Casserole Mix
¾ C. water
1 T. butter
1 T. sour cream

Preheat oven to 350°. Empty Hash Brown Casserole Mix into a mug. In small saucepan over medium heat, combine water and butter. Bring to a simmer and pour over ingredients in mug, stirring until well combined. Stir in sour cream. Cover with aluminum foil and bake for 20 to 25 minutes.

Brown Rice
Pilaf Mix

Brown Rice Pilaf Mix

½ C. instant brown rice
1 tsp. dried green bell pepper
½ tsp. dried parsley flakes
1 tsp. dried celery flakes
¼ tsp. dried onion flakes

Pinch of garlic powder
1 T. chicken gravy mix
¼ tsp. salt
Pinch of pepper
1 T. sunflower nuts

In a small bowl, combine above ingredients. Mix well, place in a sandwich-size bag and seal. Place sealed bag in a mug. Make sure the mug holds a volume of at least 1½ cups.

Decorate mug and attach a gift tag with the directions on how to prepare the pilaf.

Brown Rice Pilaf

Brown Rice Pilaf Mix
½ C. water
1 T. olive oil
2 T. milk

Preheat oven to 350°. Empty Brown Rice Pilaf Mix into a mug. In small saucepan over medium heat, combine water, oil and milk. Bring to a simmer and pour over ingredients in mug. Cover with aluminum foil and bake for 10 to 12 minutes. Let mixture stand for 5 minutes before uncovering. Fluff lightly with a fork and enjoy.

For a quality black and white reproduction, photocopy the above tag. Any of the color tags may also be photocopied for additional gifts.

Brown Rice Pilaf

Brown Rice Pilaf Mix
½ C. water
1 T. olive oil
2 T. milk

Preheat oven to 350°. Empty Brown Rice Pilaf Mix into a mug. In small saucepan over medium heat, combine water, oil and milk. Bring to a simmer and pour over ingredients in mug. Cover with aluminum foil and bake for 10 to 12 minutes. Let mixture stand for 5 minutes before uncovering. Fluff lightly with a fork and enjoy.

Brown Rice Pilaf

Brown Rice Pilaf Mix
½ C. water
1 T. olive oil
2 T. milk

Preheat oven to 350°. Empty Brown Rice Pilaf Mix into a mug. In small saucepan over medium heat, combine water, oil and milk. Bring to a simmer and pour over ingredients in mug. Cover with aluminum foil and bake for 10 to 12 minutes. Let mixture stand for 5 minutes before uncovering. Fluff lightly with a fork and enjoy.

Brown Rice Pilaf

Brown Rice Pilaf Mix
½ C. water
1 T. olive oil
2 T. milk

Preheat oven to 350°. Empty Brown Rice Pilaf Mix into a mug. In small saucepan over medium heat, combine water, oil and milk. Bring to a simmer and pour over ingredients in mug. Cover with aluminum foil and bake for 10 to 12 minutes. Let mixture stand for 5 minutes before uncovering. Fluff lightly with a fork and enjoy.

Brown Rice Pilaf

Brown Rice Pilaf Mix
½ C. water
1 T. olive oil
2 T. milk

Preheat oven to 350°. Empty Brown Rice Pilaf Mix into a mug. In small saucepan over medium heat, combine water, oil and milk. Bring to a simmer and pour over ingredients in mug. Cover with aluminum foil and bake for 10 to 12 minutes. Let mixture stand for 5 minutes before uncovering. Fluff lightly with a fork and enjoy.

Meat & Potato Pie Mix

Meat & Potato Pie Mix

1 T. brown gravy mix
½ tsp. paprika
1 tsp. dried chives
½ C. instant mashed
  potato flakes

Pinch of salt and pepper
1 tsp. dried parsley flakes
1 (5 oz.) can chunk
  chicken

In a small bowl, combine brown gravy mix, paprika and chives. Mix well, place in a sandwich-size bag and seal. In a separate bag, combine potato flakes, salt, pepper and parsley flakes; mix and seal. Place can of chicken in a mug and top with sealed bags. Make sure the mug holds a volume of at least 1½ cups.

Decorate mug and attach a gift tag with the directions on how to prepare the casserole.

Meat & Potato Pie

Meat & Potato Pie Mix
1 T. butter
½ C. milk
2 T. water

Preheat oven to 350°. In a small bowl, combine chicken from can (undrained) with contents of bag containing chives. Stir well and pour into lightly greased mug. In a small saucepan over medium heat, combine butter, milk and water. Bring to a boil and add contents from remaining bag. Mix well and pour over chicken mixture in mug. Bake for 20 to 25 minutes.

For a quality black and white reproduction, photocopy the above tag. Any of the color tags may also be photocopied for additional gifts.

Meat & Potato Pie

Meat & Potato Pie Mix
½ T. butter
¼ C. milk
1 T. water

Preheat oven to 350°. In a small bowl, combine chicken from can (undrained) with contents of bag containing chives. Stir well and pour into lightly greased mug. In a small saucepan over medium heat, combine butter, milk and water. Bring to a boil and add contents from remaining bag. Mix well and pour over chicken mixture in mug. Bake for 20 to 25 minutes.

Meat & Potato Pie

Meat & Potato Pie Mix
½ T. butter
¼ C. milk
1 T. water

Preheat oven to 350°. In a small bowl, combine chicken from can (undrained) with contents of bag containing chives. Stir well and pour into lightly greased mug. In a small saucepan over medium heat, combine butter, milk and water. Bring to a boil and add contents from remaining bag. Mix well and pour over chicken mixture in mug. Bake for 20 to 25 minutes.

Meat & Potato Pie

Meat & Potato Pie Mix
½ T. butter
¼ C. milk
1 T. water

Preheat oven to 350°. In a small bowl, combine chicken from can (undrained) with contents of bag containing chives. Stir well and pour into lightly greased mug. In a small saucepan over medium heat, combine butter, milk and water. Bring to a boil and add contents from remaining bag. Mix well and pour over chicken mixture in mug. Bake for 20 to 25 minutes.

MEAT & POTATO PIE

Meat & Potato Pie Mix
½ T. butter
¼ C. milk
1 T. water

Preheat oven to 350°. In a small bowl, combine chicken from can (undrained) with contents of bag containing chives. Stir well and pour into lightly greased mug. In a small saucepan over medium heat, combine butter, milk and water. Bring to a boil and add contents from remaining bag. Mix well and pour over chicken mixture in mug. Bake for 20 to 25 minutes.

Sweet Potato
Apple Bake Mix

Sweet Potato Apple Bake Mix

2 T. dried apples
1 T. raisins
¼ tsp. cinnamon
2 tsp. sugar

1 tsp. dried parsley flakes
1 tsp. instant chicken
bouillon

In a small bowl, combine above ingredients. Mix well, place in a sandwich-size bag and seal. Place sealed bag in a mug. Make sure the mug holds a volume of at least 1½ cups.

Decorate mug and attach a gift tag with the directions on how to prepare the recipe.

Sweet Potato Apple Bake

2 T. butter, melted
2 T. water
1 C. peeled, cubed
sweet potatoes
Sweet Potato Apple
Bake Mix

Preheat oven to 350°. In a small bowl, combine melted butter and water. Add peeled, cubed sweet potatoes and Sweet Potato Apple Bake Mix. Mix well and place mixture in lightly greased mug. Loosely cover mug with aluminum foil and bake for 24 to 28 minutes.

For a quality black and white reproduction, photocopy the above tag. Any of the color tags may also be photocopied for additional gifts.

Sweet Potato Apple Bake

2 T. butter, melted
2 T. water
1 C. peeled, cubed
   sweet potatoes
Sweet Potato Apple
   Bake Mix

Preheat oven to 350°. In a small bowl, combine melted butter and water. Add peeled, cubed sweet potatoes and Sweet Potato Apple Bake Mix. Mix well and place mixture in lightly greased mug. Loosely cover mug with aluminum foil and bake for 24 to 28 minutes.

SWEET POTATO APPLE BAKE

2 T. butter, melted
2 T. water
1 C. peeled, cubed
   sweet potatoes
Sweet Potato Apple
   Bake Mix

Preheat oven to 350°. In a small bowl, combine melted butter and water. Add peeled, cubed sweet potatoes and Sweet Potato Apple Bake Mix. Mix well and place mixture in lightly greased mug. Loosely cover mug with aluminum foil and bake for 24 to 28 minutes.

Sweet Potato Apple Bake

2 T. butter, melted
2 T. water
1 C. peeled, cubed
   sweet potatoes
Sweet Potato Apple
   Bake Mix

Preheat oven to 350°. In a small bowl, combine melted butter and water. Add peeled, cubed sweet potatoes and Sweet Potato Apple Bake Mix. Mix well and place mixture in lightly greased mug. Loosely cover mug with aluminum foil and bake for 24 to 28 minutes.

Sweet Potato Apple Bake

2 T. butter, melted
2 T. water
1 C. peeled, cubed
   sweet potatoes
Sweet Potato Apple
   Bake Mix

Preheat oven to 350°. In a small bowl, combine melted butter and water. Add peeled, cubed sweet potatoes and Sweet Potato Apple Bake Mix. Mix well and place mixture in lightly greased mug. Loosely cover mug with aluminum foil and bake for 24 to 28 minutes.

Cran-Pecan
Stuffing Mix

Cran-Pecan Stuffing Mix

1 C. dry cornbread
   stuffing mix*

1½ T. chopped pecans
½ T. dried cranberries

In a small bowl, combine above ingredients. Toss well, place in a sandwich-size bag and seal. Place sealed bag in a mug. Make sure the mug holds a volume of at least 1½ cups.

Decorate mug and attach a gift tag with the directions on how to prepare the stuffing.

If preferred, cut homemade cornbread into small cubes and oven-dry thoroughly. Mix 1 cup dry cornbread cubes, ½ teaspoon dried onion flakes and 1 teaspoon each dried celery flakes and instant chicken bouillon. Then add pecans and cranberries as directed.

Cran-Pecan Stuffing

Cran-Pecan Stuffing Mix
1½ T. butter
½ C. water

Preheat oven to 350°. Empty Cran-Pecan Stuffing Mix into a small bowl. In a glass measuring cup, combine butter and water. Heat in microwave until butter is melted; pour over ingredients in bowl and toss well. Place mixture in lightly greased mug. Cover mug with aluminum foil and bake for 20 minutes. Uncover and bake 2 minutes more. Let cool slightly before enjoying.

For a quality black and white reproduction, photocopy the above tag. Any of the color tags may also be photocopied for additional gifts.

Cran-Pecan Stuffing

Cran-Pecan Stuffing Mix
1½ T. butter
½ C. water

Preheat oven to 350°. Empty Cran-Pecan Stuffing Mix into a small bowl. In a glass measuring cup, combine butter and water. Heat in microwave until butter is melted; pour over ingredients in bowl and toss well. Place mixture in lightly greased mug. Cover mug with aluminum foil and bake for 20 minutes. Uncover and bake 2 minutes more. Let cool slightly before enjoying.

CRAN-PECAN STUFFING

Cran-Pecan Stuffing Mix
1½ T. butter
½ C. water

Preheat oven to 350°. Empty Cran-Pecan Stuffing Mix into a small bowl. In a glass measuring cup, combine butter and water. Heat in microwave until butter is melted; pour over ingredients in bowl and toss well. Place mixture in lightly greased mug. Cover mug with aluminum foil and bake for 20 minutes. Uncover and bake 2 minutes more. Let cool slightly before enjoying.

Cran-Pecan Stuffing

Cran-Pecan Stuffing Mix
1½ T. butter
½ C. water

Preheat oven to 350°. Empty Cran-Pecan Stuffing Mix into a small bowl. In a glass measuring cup, combine butter and water. Heat in microwave until butter is melted; pour over ingredients in bowl and toss well. Place mixture in lightly greased mug. Cover mug with aluminum foil and bake for 20 minutes. Uncover and bake 2 minutes more. Let cool slightly before enjoying.

Cran-Pecan Stuffing

Cran-Pecan Stuffing Mix
1½ T. butter
½ C. water

Preheat oven to 350°. Empty Cran-Pecan Stuffing Mix into a small bowl. In a glass measuring cup, combine butter and water. Heat in microwave until butter is melted; pour over ingredients in bowl and toss well. Place mixture in lightly greased mug. Cover mug with aluminum foil and bake for 20 minutes. Uncover and bake 2 minutes more. Let cool slightly before enjoying.

Index

Brown Rice Pilaf 43

Chicken & Rice Casserole 3

Cran-Pecan Stuffing 55

Currant Almond Rice 27

Golden Fruit Compote 19

Grits & Cheese Casserole 23

Hash Brown Casserole 39

Hearty Ranch Potatoes 7

Hot Chicken Salad Casserole 35

Meat & Potato Pie 47

Mexican Lasagna 15

Nutty Oatmeal 11

Pecan Chicken & Rice Salad 31

Sweet Potato Apple Bake 51

Mug'ems

Collect all 3!

Mug'ems Meals

Give'em & Bake'em ✦ Recipes in a Mug!

Mug'ems *Sweet Things*

Give'em & Bake'em ✦ Recipes in a Mug!

Mug'ems *Soups & Breads*

Give'em & Bake'em ✦ Recipes in a Mug!

Create yummy gifts from your kitchen!